Devotions to the
Holy Spirit

Brian Moore, SJ

Pauline

BOOKS & MEDIA

Boston

Imprimi Potest: Patrick O'Sullivan, SJ,
                                    Provincial
Nihil Obstat: William Dougherty
                                    Censor Deputatus
Imprimatur: James Madden
                                    Vicar General
                                    Sydney, November 10, 1976

Devotion to the Holy Spirit

First Edition:
St. Paul Publication—Homebush NSW Australia

American Edition, 1988

Printed and published in the U.S.A. by Pauline Books &
Media, 50 Saint Pauls Avenue, Boston MA 02130-3491.

www.pauline.org

Pauline Books & Media is the publishing house of the
Daughters of St. Paul, an international congregation of
women religious serving the Church with the communica-
tions media.

Acknowledgment

The prayers in this collection are, for the most part, the author's own, or his translation. Exceptions have been acknowledged. Prayers whose origin he has been unable to determine are classified as anonymous. Those prayers which were formerly indulgenced are noted as traditional.

Contents

Introduction

Daily and Occasional Prayers

Additional Prayers

Practices

The Holy Spirit in Our Lives

The Christian's "spiritual life" is precisely that—"spiritual"; that is to say, a life lived in the Spirit, who has made his home in us (Rom 8:9). It is this Holy Spirit, living in us and in whom we live, who enables us to call God our Father (cf. Rom 8:15), to proclaim "Jesus is Lord" (cf. 1 Cor 12:3), to put an end to the misdeeds of the body (cf. Rom 8:13). It is the Holy Spirit who enables us to understand the wisdom of God (1 Cor 2:10), who supports us in our weakness and who, when we do not know what to say, himself prays for us (cf. Rom 8:26).

All of us have been washed in the Spirit of God (cf. 1 Cor 6:11) and given to drink of the one Spirit (cf. 1 Cor 12:13). We are all one body in Christ. It is through the working of the Holy Spirit that, from age to age, the Father gathers us to himself in Christ. The Holy Spirit is the Spirit of fellowship; the one Soul animating the one Body of Christ, which is the Church.

Led by the Spirit

Christ our Lord, the Son of God, was, as man, led by the Spirit of God. It was by the Spirit that he was led into the wilderness to be put to the test (cf. Mt 4:1); that he cast out the powers of evil (cf. Mt 12:28); that he spoke in the synagogue at Nazareth (cf. Lk 4:14-18); that he chose his apostles (cf. Acts 1:2).

What is true of the Son of God is true also of all the children of God. They who are children of God, says St. Paul, are led by the Spirit of God (cf. Rom 8:14). By these words we are taught two things:

a) That we, who have been adopted by God as his children, have the *right* to call upon the Holy Spirit to come to us, to lead us, to enlighten us, to teach us, and to love us;

b) that, being children of God, we have the *duty* to show in our lives visible signs that the Holy Spirit is our Guide.

When we claim our right to the help of the Holy Spirit, we are asking, in scriptural terms, for the "Seven Gifts of the Holy Spirit." We are asking for *Wisdom*—for that wisdom of God which shows mere human wisdom to be folly (cf. 1 Cor 1:19-31); *Understanding*—that is, spiritual insight which guards us against spiritual shallowness; *Counsel*—which is a maturity of judgment guarding us against imprudent action or judgment; *Knowledge* of the things of God and his ways with men; *Fortitude*—the kind of courage which "bears all things, hopes all things, sustains all things"; *Piety*—that deep sense of reverence for God in all his wonder; and *Fear of the Lord*—the fear one has who is deeply in love and greatly loved, and fears to do anything that will diminish that love in any way (cf. Is 11:1-5).

"By their fruits you will know them," says our Lord. When we try to be and to live as children of God, we are in fact trying to make our lives full of the "fruits of the Holy Spirit." These "fruits" are the visible evidence of the invisible indwelling of the Holy Spirit within us.

And the greatest of these is *love.*

The Spirit of Love

"Unless the Holy Spirit," writes St. Augustine, "were so given to each one of us as to make each of us one who loves both God and neighbor, no one could be transferred from the left hand of God to the right. The reason why the Spirit is rightly called the 'Gift' is simply love. Love, then, which is of God, and is God, is properly the Holy Spirit—through whom the love of God is poured out into our hearts (cf. Rom 5:5); and through that love the whole Trinity dwells in us. Rightly then is the Holy Spirit, who is God, also called the Gift of God."

Charity, then, love of God and of our neighbor, is the most excellent fruit of the Holy Spirit's indwelling; and the way of love is the more excellent way (cf. 1 Cor 12:31—13:1-13).

Charity is the fountainhead of all the other fruits of the Holy Spirit's action in us— *joy, peace, patience, kindness, goodness, long-suffering, gentleness, faith, modesty, self-control, chastity*—as St. Paul writes to the Galatians (5:22), contrasting a life lived in the Spirit with the kind of behavior that belongs to the flesh: "Now the works of the flesh are plain: fornication, impurity, licentiousness, idolatry, sorcery, enmity, strife, jealousy, anger, selfishness, dissension, party spirit, envy, drunkenness, carousing, and the like" (Gal 5:19-21 RSV).

St. Paul, in this same letter, puts the matter in a nutshell: if the Spirit is the source of our life, let the Spirit also direct the course of our life (cf. Gal 5:25).

Devotions are said to be the temptation of the devout. True devotion to the Holy Spirit consists above all in being docile to his guidance, open to his action in us, attentive to his inspiration as he leads us to avoid evil and do good.

Sanctifying the Day

Morning

Holy Spirit, at creation's first dawn
you came forth to give form and life to all;
hear me at the beginning of this new day.
Shape my life today in the image of Christ;
let nothing unpleasant be found in me.
Illumine my life's horizon with your light;
dispel all darkness from my mind and soul;
light the fire of love in my heart;
and be the light I radiate today,
and every day of my life.

Midday

Higher than the midday sun may you rise,
Flame of Love, in my heart;
brighter than the midday sun may you shine,
Divine Light, in my soul;
warmer than the midday sun may you burn,
Pentecostal Fire, in my mind.
Irradiate, holy Light, our world;
inflame, Divine Fire, our hearts;
prevail, Love's Power, over our wills.

Evening

At the setting of the sun,
to you, unfailing Light, I turn.
I thank you for the day now fading,
and pray you give
an evening of quiet to my spirit.
Let me rest in you that I may know
refreshment of soul, and peace of heart.
Silent and still, attentive to you alone,
let my soul breathe
no other breath than you, O Holy Spirit.

Night

In stillness and in silence as deep as night,
may my soul be before you, Holy Spirit.
Come down upon me, soft as the starlight;
close around me, closer than the dark;
refresh me and renew me,
as dewfall and rainfall renew the earth.
Stay with me, Lord, until the morning comes;
and at the dawning of the new day
be an even brighter sunburst
in my soul.

Prayer Before Confession

Holy Spirit, my Creator and my Lord,
by my sins I both resist and grieve you;
and I misuse this temple of yours.
Shed upon me the radiance of your light
that I may see my sin for what it truly is.
Move my mind and heart by your great power
that I may be truly sorry
and firmly decided to amend.
Wash away my sins
and in the fire of your love consume
everything in me
which is displeasing to you.

Prayer After Confession

Holy Spirit, Giver of all good things,
accept the thanks I offer you
for your gift of pardon and of peace,
and the joy I have in you who live in me.
Let me live in praise of your mercy and love
by which I am set free from my sins
and given the sure hope of seeing you
face to face in the glory of eternal life.
Until that day dawns, abide in me
that I may live and move
only on the impulse of your love.

Prayer Before Communion

Holy Spirit, by your powerful grace
you prepared the virgin heart of Mary
to receive the Word of God made flesh.
At the touch of your transforming fire
the gifts we laid upon this altar have become
the very Body and Blood of Christ.
Breathe also on me; work within me,
so that I may become one soul with Christ—
my Savior with whom you and the Father
are one only God and Lord.

Prayer After Communion

Holy Spirit, be my only Guide.
Jesus, present now within me,
has made me one with himself;
teach me
to submit myself to you as he did
in all things,
to follow wherever you lead me,
to answer whenever you call me,
to listen whenever you speak within me.

Novena of Prayers to the Holy Spirit

During the nine days between the Ascension of our Lord and the coming of his promised Gift, the Holy Spirit, the followers of Jesus were gathered in prayer, together with Mary, the Mother of Jesus.

Come Holy Spirit: fill the hearts of your
    faithful;
and enkindle in them the fire of your love.
Send forth your Spirit, O Lord, and they
    shall be created;
and you will renew the face of the earth.
Glory be to the Father...

"Veni Creator" (page 37) or "Veni Sancte Spiritus" (page 38).

Prayers of the Day follow (pages 18-26).

And then:

The love of God is poured into our hearts,
Alleluia!
Through his Spirit who lives in us,
Alleluia!

O God,
you teach the hearts of the faithful
through the light of the Holy Spirit:
grant that,
through that same Holy Spirit,
we may have a right understanding

in all things,
and always rejoice in his consolations.
Through Christ our Lord. Amen.

or

Lord, may the power of the Holy Spirit
be in us
to cleanse our hearts
and to keep us safe from all harm.
Through Christ our Lord. Amen.

or

Lord,
be gracious to us
and pour into our hearts that Holy Spirit
by whose wisdom we were created
and by whose loving care we are aided.
Through Christ our Lord. Amen.

Traditional

Prayer: First Day

Come,
You who best console the lonely heart,
Refuge in danger, Protector in distress.
Come,
You who cleanse the soul of every stain,
and heal all its wounds.
Come,
Strength of the weak,
Support of those on the verge of falling.
Come,
Teacher of those who are humble of heart,
who humbles the proud-hearted.
Come,
Father of the fatherless, Hope of the poor,
Treasure of those in need.
Come,
guiding Star of every pilgrim,
Harbor for those in danger of shipwreck.
Come,
Strength of the living,
Salvation of those about to die.
Come,
Holy Spirit,
and have mercy on me.

St. Augustine

Prayer: Second Day

Breathe in me, O Holy Spirit,
that my thoughts may all be holy.
Act in me, O Holy Spirit,
that my work, too, may be holy.
Draw my heart, O Holy Spirit,
that I may love only what is holy.
Strengthen me, O Holy Spirit,
that I may defend all that is holy.
Guard me, O Holy Spirit,
that I may always be holy.

St. Augustine

Holy Spirit, love of my heart,
I adore you.
Enlighten me, guide me,
strengthen me, console me.
Tell me what I must do—
command me.
I promise to submit myself
to all that you will of me,
and accept all you permit to befall me.
Let me only know your will.

Cardinal Mercier

Prayer: Third Day

Most Holy Spirit, the Paraclete,
behold me prostrate before you.
Most profoundly do I adore you,
most thankfully bless you.
With the countless Seraphim
who stand before your throne,
I, too, cry out, "Holy, Holy, Holy."
I firmly believe that you are God,
one with the Father and the Son.
I hope that in your goodness
you will sanctify and save my soul.
I love you, divine Love, with all my heart
and above all that this world holds—
because you alone, Infinite Goodness,
are worthy of all love.
In my blindness and ingratitude,
I have often offended you by my sins.
I ask your forgiveness.
I offer you this heart of mine—
cold and dark:
I pray you, shed your light upon it;
warm it with the fire of your love.

St. Alphonsus Liguori (adapted)

Prayer: Fourth Day

Holy Spirit, Lord and Giver of life,
you who came down upon the apostles
in a mighty wind and with fire,
who filled the house where they were and
gave them the gift of tongues
to proclaim the wonders of God,
come down now upon me also.
Fill me with yourself;
and make of me a temple wherein you dwell.
Open my lips to proclaim your praise,
to ask your guidance,
and to declare your love.
Holy Light, divine Fire, eternal Might,
enlighten my mind to know you,
inflame my heart to love you,
strengthen my will to seek and find you.
Be for me
the living and life-giving Breath of God,
the very air I breathe,
and the only sky in which my spirit soars.

Prayer: Fifth Day

O Holy Spirit,
Divine Spirit of light and of love,
to you I consecrate
my understanding, my heart and my will,
and my whole being,
in time and in eternity.
May my understanding always be submissive
to your heavenly inspirations
and to the teachings of the holy Church
of which you are the infallible Guide.
May my heart be ever on fire
with the love of my God and my neighbor.
May my will be always in harmony with
the will of God.
And may my whole life be a faithful copy
of the life and virtues
of our Lord and Savior, Jesus Christ—
to whom, with the Father and with you,
be honor and glory forever.

Traditional

Prayer: Sixth Day

Holy Spirit with the Father and the Son
grant that the whole universe
may be consecrated to you,
and that there may not be a single heart
in which you,
who are Love, Union and Peace,
do not reign.
Holy Spirit, Creator,
look with favor upon the Church,
and by your heavenly power
make it strong and secure
against the attacks of its enemies.
Renew in charity and in grace
the spirit of your servants,
whom you have anointed,
that they may give glory to you,
with the Father
and his only-begotten Son.
Holy Spirit, Spirit of Truth,
come into our hearts;
shed the brightness of your light
upon all nations,
that all may be one in faith,
and pleasing to you.

Traditional

Prayer: Seventh Day

Holy Spirit,
infinite Love of the Father and the Son,
through the hands of Mary,
your immaculate spouse,
and upon the altar of the Heart of Jesus,
I offer you myself today
and every day of my life.
I offer you, my Lord, my daily labors:
may they be fragrant
with the spirit of love of the cross.
I offer you my life and my death,
my head and my hands,
my every step, my every breath,
all the love of my soul
and every beat of my heart.
And I firmly resolve
faithfully to hear your voice,
and, in all things, to do your will.

Anonymous (adapted)

Prayer: Eighth Day

Upon my knees before you,
in the sight of the whole heavenly court,
I offer myself, body and soul,
to you, eternal Spirit.
I adore you for your great glory;
I rejoice in the splendor of your majesty
and wonder at the might of your love.
You are the light and strength of my soul;
in you I live and move and am.
I never want to grieve you
by unfaithfulness to your grace,
and I pray you
keep me from every stain of sin.
Make me faithful to you in everything,
at all times.
Grant that I may always
listen to your voice and obey.
Grant that I may always
watch for your light
and follow the leading of your grace.
To you do I cling,
and ask you in your mercy
to watch over me in my weakness.

Anonymous (adapted)

Prayer: Ninth Day

Holy Spirit, Spirit of Jesus
who anointed him
at his baptism by John,
who anointed with Pentecostal fire
the Church, which is his Body,
descend upon the Church, and upon all
who have been consecrated to you—
all who received you in Baptism,
all who were sealed by you in Confirmation,
all who have been set aside
by you through the priesthood
to serve God and humanity.
Renew in us all the graces
by which we have been sanctified,
washed clean of our sins,
and made temples of your indwelling.
Let us no longer grieve you
by our faithlessness or indifference,
but rather, filled with your fire,
let us love you with that love
which is poured out in our hearts
by your coming to us.

Novena of Readings and Reflections

The Novena of Readings and Reflections may also be combined with the Novena of Prayers found on pages 16-26.

Before reading the selected passages from Scripture, pause for a few moments and direct your thoughts in love and obedience to the Holy Spirit who dwells within you.

Opening Prayer

Open my heart, Holy Spirit, to receive your word. Make my will strong, Holy Spirit, to follow wherever you lead.

Read the day's passage slowly and thoughtfully in company with the Holy Spirit who inspired its writing.

Concluding Prayer

I thank you, Holy Spirit, for your word.
Make it a living reality in my life—
a constant guide at my side, a lamp for
my feet and a light for my path.

First Day

Beloved, do not be surprised at the fiery ordeal which comes upon you to prove you, as though something strange were happening to you. But rejoice insofar as you share Christ's sufferings, that you may also rejoice and be glad when his glory is revealed. If you are reproached for the name of Christ, you are blessed, because the spirit of glory and of God rests upon you. If one suffers as a Christian, let him not be ashamed, but under that name let him glorify God.

1 Peter 4:12-14, 17

Reflection

Do I try to penetrate the mystery of suffering? Do I believe that the trials of this life are a sharing in the passion of Christ? Do I see the Spirit who raised Jesus from the dead permeating every human suffering? Am I fearlessly Christian in my daily life?

Second Day

For we ourselves were once foolish, disobedient, led astray, slaves to various passions and pleasures, passing our day in malice and envy, hated by men and hating one another; but when the goodness and loving kindness of God our Savior appeared, he saved us, not because of deeds done by us in righteousness, but in virtue of his own mercy, by the washing of regeneration and renewal in the Holy Spirit which he poured out upon us richly through Jesus Christ our Savior, so that we might be justified by his grace and become heirs in hope of eternal life.

Titus 3:3-8

Reflection

Do I understand what I would be without Christ and his Spirit? How much am I still like that despite all God's goodness to me? Do I nurture anxieties not in keeping with the sure hope of eternal life? Am I content to leave things to God?

Third Day

Be at peace among yourselves. And we exhort you, brethren, admonish the idlers, encourage the fainthearted, help the weak, be patient with them all. See that none of you repays evil for evil, but always seek to do good to one another and to all. Rejoice always, pray constantly, give thanks in all circumstances; for this is the will of God in Christ Jesus for you. Do not quench the Spirit, do not despise prophesying, but test everything; hold fast what is good, abstain from every form of evil.

May the God of peace himself sanctify you wholly; and may your spirit and soul and body be kept sound and blameless at the coming of our Lord Jesus Christ.

1 Thessalonians 4:13-23

Reflection

Which are more dominant in my life: the fruits of the Holy Spirit or their opposites (see page 10)? Do I sincerely try to acquire these fruits, really desire to possess them, pray to have them?

Fourth Day

When anything is exposed by the light it becomes visible, or anything that becomes visible is light. Therefore it is said,
"Awake, O sleeper, and arise from
    the dead,
and Christ shall give you light."

Look carefully then how you walk, not as unwise men, but as wise, making the most of the time, because the days are evil. Therefore do not be foolish, but understand what the will of the Lord is. And do not get drunk with wine, for this is debauchery; but be filled with the Spirit, addressing one another in psalms and hymns and spiritual songs, singing and making melody to the Lord with all your heart, always and for everything giving thanks in the name of our Lord Jesus Christ to God the Father.

Ephesians 5:13-20

Reflection

Is my heart as joyful as a Christian heart should be? Do I really try to discover what God's will is for me? How much of my prayer is thanksgiving to God?

Fifth Day

I bow my knees before the Father, from whom every family in heaven and on earth is named, that according to the riches of his glory he may grant you to be strengthened with might through his Spirit in the inner man, and that Christ may dwell in your hearts through faith; that you, being rooted and grounded in love, may have power to comprehend with all the saints what is the breadth and length and height and depth, and to know the love of Christ which surpasses knowledge, that you may be filled with all the fullness of God.

Ephesians 3:14-19

Reflection

Within me, the indwelling Trinity is at work. Through the Spirit who proceeds from both, the Father is forming the image of Christ within me, so that he may love me as he loves his Son. What obstacles do I place in his way?

Sixth Day

All these [spiritual gifts] are inspired by one and the same Spirit, who apportions to each one individually as he wills.

For just as the body is one and has many members, and all the members of the body, though many, are one body, so it is with Christ. For by one Spirit we were all baptized into one body—Jews or Greeks, slaves or free—and all were made to drink of one Spirit.

1 Corinthians 12:11-13

Reflection

For what do I usually use the gifts of God: for his glory? for the good of others? or for my own self? How actively do I promote a oneness of body and spirit in my home, community, church? In what ways am I a cause of division?

Seventh Day

Do you not know that you are God's temple and that God's Spirit dwells in you? If anyone destroys God's temple, God will destroy him. For God's temple is holy, and that temple you are.

Let no one deceive himself. If any one among you thinks that he is wise in this age, let him become a fool that he may become wise. For the wisdom of this world is folly with God. For it is written, "He catches the wise in their craftiness," and again, "The Lord knows that the thoughts of the wise are futile." So let no one boast of men. For all things are yours...and you are Christ's; and Christ is God's.

1 Corinthians 3:16-23

Reflection

Do I really see myself as a temple of God? Am I wise—seeing, judging, weighing all things in the light of eternal reality? Am I willing to belong entirely to Christ as he belongs to God?

Eighth Day

For the Spirit searches everything, even the depths of God. For what person knows a man's thoughts except the spirit of the man which is in him? So also no one comprehends the thoughts of God except the Spirit of God. Now we have received not the spirit of the world, but the Spirit which is from God, that we might understand the gifts bestowed on us by God. And we impart this in words not taught by human wisdom but taught by the Spirit, interpreting spiritual truths to those who possess the Spirit.

1 Corinthians 2:10-13

Reflection

Do I try to see myself as I really am—in the light of the Holy Spirit? If I did, would it make me rely wholly, always and only on the Holy Spirit? Do I see all that I am and have, and all that happens to me and others, only in the light of the Holy Spirit?

Ninth Day

We know that the whole creation has been groaning in travail together until now; and not only the creation, but we ourselves, who have the first fruits of the Spirit, groan inwardly as we wait for adoption as sons, the redemption of our bodies.

The Spirit helps us in our weakness; for we do not know how to pray as we ought, but the Spirit himself intercedes for us with sighs too deep for words. And he who searches the hearts of men knows what is the mind of the Spirit, because the Spirit intercedes for the saints according to the will of God.

Romans 8:22-23, 26-27

Reflection

Do my mind and heart possess the serenity and confidence that come from knowing the Spirit intercedes for me? Am I willing to pray only according to the will of God? Do I ask the help of the Holy Spirit in my prayer?

Veni Creator

Come, Spirit, our Creator, come
And in your servants live;
To hearts that you yourself have made
Your grace from heaven give.

You are the one who pleads for us
The Gift of God—our goal;
Love's Self, and Fire, and Source of Life,
And healing strength of soul.

God's Finger writing in our hearts,
And seven times a Gift,
You are the Father's Promise true:
Our speech enrich, uplift.

A flame to guide our senses, light;
With love our hearts secure.
Supply for failings of our flesh
With power to endure.

Still farther yet drive back our foe,
And soon give us your peace;
With you before us leading on
From all wrong may we cease.

Through you may we the Father know,
And learn through you the Son,
Believing now and evermore,
That both with you are one.

All glory to the Father be,
And to his risen Son;
All glory, Spirit, be to you
While endless ages run.

Veni Sancte Spiritus

Holy Spirit, God of Love,
Come, and let fall from above
Ray of your light.

Father, come to those in need,
Come, rewarding every deed,
Light of our hearts.

You the one who best consoles,
You most welcome Guest of souls,
Refuge and rest.

Respite in the toil of life,
Subduer of the passions' strife,
Comfort in grief.

Light, which blessedness imparts,
Fill the inmost core of hearts
Faithful and true.

In your absence all is pain,
Man's endeavor all in vain,
Harmful all things.

What is soiled, wash again;
What is arid, bless with rain;
What wounded, heal.

Warm again the love grown cold;
What unyielding, shape and mold;
What wayward, rule.

Give, to faithful hearts confessing,
gifts beyond all else possessing
Sevenfold worth.

Crown the strivings of the soul;
Give, when we have reached the goal,
Joy evermore.

In Every Need

Holy Spirit,
my Light, my Life, my Love, my Strength,
be with me now, and always:
in all my doubts, anxieties and trials,
come, Holy Spirit;
in hours of loneliness, weariness and grief,
come, Holy Spirit;
in failure, in loss and in disappointment,
come, Holy Spirit;
when others fail me, when I fail myself,
come, Holy Spirit;
when I am ill, unable to work, depressed,
come, Holy Spirit;
now, and forever, and in all things,
come, Holy Spirit.

General Intercessions to the Holy Spirit

Come, Holy Spirit, upon the Church:
strengthen and enlighten her
so that she may work effectively
for the salvation of all mankind.
Come, Holy Spirit.

Come, Holy Spirit, give counsel and wisdom
to our Holy Father the Pope
and to all the bishops
to guide your flock.
Come, Holy Spirit.

Come, Holy Spirit, give to your people
the outpouring of your grace:
teach, console and enlighten
all to whom you have been given.
Come, Holy Spirit.

Come, Holy Spirit, cleanse our hearts
    of all hatred,
and fill us with love toward everyone.
Come, Holy Spirit.

Come, Holy Spirit, enlighten those who
    govern us.
May they see what is right
and in your strength have the courage
to do what is right.
Come, Holy Spirit.

Come, Holy Spirit, Bond of unity and peace.
Hasten the unity of all people in Christ;
take from our midst the scourge of war,
and from our hearts the cause of war.
Come, Holy Spirit.

Come, Holy Spirit, descend upon all
who have been baptized into Christ:
break down the barriers which divide us,
and strengthen the bonds which unite us.
Make all one in faith and love.
Come, Holy Spirit.

Come, Holy Spirit, and in your kindness
heal the sick, receive the dying,
counsel the doubtful,
console those who have lost hope.
May all hearts rest in you.
Come, Holy Spirit.

For Wisdom

Holy Spirit,
who with the Father and the Son,
in the beginning hovered over
the deep and formless void to give it shape,
and breathed the breath of life
into humanity, and every living creature:
come now from heaven,
from your throne of glory, come.
Be with me and help me; work with me
and teach me what is pleasing to you.
You, who know all things, guide me
to be prudent in all my undertakings;
and protect me by your glory.
Only then will everything I do
be acceptable in your sight.

Cf. Wisdom 9

For Charity

Holy Spirit, Love's own Fire,
fill our hearts with
love of God and neighbor.
Without that twofold love,
we cannot be pleasing to you;
without it no other gift avails.
Give us a love which is patient, kind,
never jealous, boastful or conceited;
a love which does not seek its own,
is not easily provoked, thinks no evil,
does not rejoice at injury done to another,
but delights in the truth.
Give us a love which bears all things,
believes all things, hopes all things,
endures all things.
Give us faith and hope;
but above all and in all, give us love.

Cf. 1 Corinthians 13

Self-Offering

Holy Spirit, God of Love,
be present to me;
accept the offering of myself
which I make to you.
Receive these hands, these feet, these eyes,
this tongue, and all my senses.
Receive
my memory, my will, my understanding,
my desires, my sighs, the longings
and the aspirations of my soul.
Receive my every hour, my every moment,
and all the happenings of my life.

Holy Spirit, God of Love,
knit my soul to you.
Let your love possess my whole being—
my senses, my powers, my affections,
my very life.
Let your love rule my labor and my rest,
my going and my staying,
and move me as it pleases.
Let your love disquiet or comfort me,
humble or exalt me,
and burn away all my faults.

Holy Spirit, God of Love,
draw me to yourself.
Do with me what you will.
Nothing will cause me fear
if only your love enfolds me.

I ask confidently
because your desire to give
is greater than mine to receive.
Transform me into yourself,
so that I may no longer know myself,
nor find myself,
except in you.

Thomas of Jesus (adapted)

For Purity of Heart

Burn within us, Holy Fire,
so that, chaste in body
and pure of heart,
we may desire to see God.

For the Gift of Prayer

Gift of the Father given in Jesus' name,
Holy Spirit of God, come into our hearts
and teach us to say, "Abba, Father."
Teach us to proclaim, "Jesus is Lord."
Teach us to love God and to cling to him
through you, Spirit of Love,
who has been poured into our hearts.
And when our own prayers fail us,
you who know the will of God,
yourself pray within us, for us.

Cf. Galatians 4; 1 Corinthians 12;
Romans 5, 8

For the Dying

Holy Spirit,
be present to all who are dying:
sustain them by your power;
console them by your love.
Even in their sufferings
fill them with your joy.
when their eyes
close to the things of this world,
grant that they may open them again on you,
unfailing Light.
And grant that, losing this world,
they may gain all things,
resting in the eternal possession of you.

For One's Friends

Holy Spirit, Love of the Father and the Son,
hear my prayer for all those
whom you have given me to love.
By the love you have for them
I pray you,
protect them from all harm,
deliver them from evil,
comfort them in sorrow,
reassure them in anxiety,
give them your own gladness,
and draw them to yourself.

For Unity

One only Spirit of Father and Son
in whom all are baptized,
of whom all have drunk;
one Giver of many gifts,
one Tree of many fruits,
one Speaker of every tongue,
renew in our day
the wonders of Pentecost.
Grant that people of every race and nation
may understand one another,
and, as one, proclaim
the praises of God.
Grant that all may be one
as you, Spirit, with the Father and the Son
are one God, one Lord.
Grant unity to the Body of Christ;
grant unity to the human family.
Sole breath of every living thing,
may all be one who, in you,
live and move and have their being.

To the Father,
for the Gift of the Spirit

O God,
you teach the hearts of the faithful
by the light of the Holy Spirit:
grant that,
through the same Holy Spirit,
we may have a right understanding
in all things,
and always rejoice in his consolations.
Through Christ our Lord.

We pray you, Lord,
may the power of the Holy Spirit be in us
to cleanse our hearts
and to keep us from all harm.
Through Christ our Lord.

We pray you, Lord, be gracious to us,
and pour into our hearts that Holy Spirit
by whose wisdom we were created
and by whose loving care we are governed.
Through Christ our Lord.

O God,
to you every heart lies open,
every will speaks,
nothing is hidden.
By the inpouring of the Holy Spirit
purify our thoughts and our hearts
so that we may love you perfectly

and praise you worthily.
Through Christ our Lord.

(trans. from Breviarium Romanum)

To the Father,
for the Gift of the Spirit

Lord, fill our minds and hearts
with the fire of the Holy Spirit
so that we may serve you
in purity of body
and please you
in cleanness of heart.
Through Christ our Lord.

Lord, may the Paraclete
who proceeds from you
enlighten our minds,
and lead us to all truth,
as your Son has promised.
Through Christ our Lord.

Lord, may the Holy Spirit
cleanse our consciences by his coming,
so that when your Son
our Lord Jesus Christ comes
he may find in us
a dwelling place prepared for him.
Through Christ our Lord.

(trans. from Breviarium Romanum)

To Jesus, for the Gift of the Spirit

Lord Jesus,
on the night of your Last Supper
you promised to ask your Father
to send us another Paraclete,
the Spirit of Truth
to abide in us and to guide us.
After ascending into heaven
you poured out upon your apostles
the Spirit of our adoption as children.
Send your Spirit, Lord Jesus, upon us—
a Spirit of wisdom and understanding,
of counsel and of knowledge,
of fortitude and of piety,
and of holy fear of the Lord—
that same Spirit who rested upon you,
anointed you,
and sent you to preach the good news
to the poor.
Inspired by that same Holy Spirit, Lord,
may our concern for all who are in need
reveal us, too, as children of God
and co-heirs with you
in the fellowship of the Holy Spirit.

To Mary,
Spouse of the Spirit

Daughter of the Most High,
Mother of God,
faithful Spouse of the Holy Spirit—
yet also
Mary of Nazareth,
Joseph's wife,
my mother—
hear my prayer for grace, O Full of Grace.
Pray your Spouse the Holy Spirit
to come upon me—
to shelter me from all ill,
to strengthen me to do what is right,
to teach me all truth.
Pray him come to me,
and abide with me,
and be within me a fountain
springing up unto eternal life.
May he sustain me in sorrow,
sanctify me in life,
and receive me at the hour of my death.
Holy Mary, Mother of God,
pray for me.

To Mary,
Spouse of the Spirit

Hail, Mother of mercy,
Mother of God, and Mother of pardon,
Mother of hope, and Mother of grace,
Mother, full of holy joy—
O Mary!

Hail, happy Virgin-Mother,
for he who sits at the Father's right hand
and rules over the heavens, earth and sky,
enclosed himself in your womb—
O Mary!

The Uncreated Father made you,
the Holy Spirit overshadowed you,
the only-begotten Son became man in you:
divine was your making—
O Mary!

Be our consolation;
O Virgin, be our joy;
and after this our exile
bring us to our heavenly home—
O Mary!

Salve, Mater Misericordiae

Celebration of the Word

The following celebration of the Word in honor of the Holy Spirit is suitable for either community or private use.

Each reading from Sacred Scripture is followed by a period of silence, and these reflective silences are the very heart of the celebration, and may be prolonged at will. Some suggestions have been made for using the time of reflection, but they are only suggestions.

In addition to the ones given here, suitable readings abound in the Scriptures. See, for example, A Novena of Readings and Reflections *(pages 27-36)* or A Month of Daily Readings *(pages 63-64)*.

So, too, other suitable hymns may readily be found.

Opening Hymn

"Veni Creator" (page 37) or some other suitable prayer or hymn.

Pause in silence for a while, remembering that it is the Spirit who prays in us, and it is he who has brought us to this prayer. Alone, we are like our Lord, led by the Spirit into the wilderness. As a group, it is through the working of the Holy Spirit that God gathers us together.

Reflect on the presence of the Spirit—in all things, in my own soul, in the Word of God which he himself has inspired.

First Reading   Ezekiel 36:24-28

The nations will know that I am the Lord, says the Lord God, when through you I vindicate my holiness before their eyes. For I will take you from the nations, and gather you from all the countries, and bring you into your own land. I will sprinkle clean water upon you, and you shall be clean from all your uncleannesses, and from all your idols I will cleanse you. A new heart I will give you, and a new spirit I will put within you; and I will take out of your flesh the heart of stone and give you a heart of flesh. And I will put my spirit within you, and cause you to walk in my statutes and be careful to observe my ordinances. You shall dwell in the land which I gave to your fathers; and you shall be my people, and I will be your God.

Pause in silence. Ask yourself: Am I a sign to the world that God, who makes the human heart holy, is at work in me? Is mine a heart of stone—or one of flesh, docile to the guidance of the Holy Spirit? Do I really want to be different—to be cleansed of all my sinfulness, to

*live a daily newness of spirit? Ask God to do as
he has promised, and promise him that you will
not place obstacles in his way.*

Responsorial Psalm 51

Have mercy on me, O God, according to
your steadfast love;
  according to your abundant mercy blot
  out my transgressions.
Wash me thoroughly from my iniquity,
  and cleanse me from my sin!

For I know my transgressions,
  and my sin is ever before me.
Against you, you only, have I sinned,
  and done that which is evil in your sight,
so that you are justified in your sentence
  and blameless in your judgment.
Behold, I was brought forth in iniquity,
  and in sin did my mother conceive me.

Behold, you desire truth in the inward being;
  therefore teach me wisdom in my secret
  heart.
Purge me with hyssop, and I shall be clean;
  wash me, and I shall be whiter than
  snow.
Fill me with joy and gladness;
  let the bones which you have broken
  rejoice.

Hide your face from my sins,
   and blot out all my iniquities.

Create in me a clean heart, O God,
   and put a new and right spirit within me.
Cast me not away from your presence,
   and take not your holy Spirit from me.
Restore to me the joy of your salvation,
   and uphold me with a willing spirit.

Then I will teach transgressors your ways,
   and sinners will return to you.
Deliver me from bloodguiltiness, O God,
   the God of my salvation,
   and my tongue will sing aloud of your
      deliverance.

O Lord, open my lips,
   and my mouth shall show forth your
      praise.
For you have no delight in sacrifice;
   were I to give a burnt offering, you
      would not be pleased.
The sacrifice acceptable to God is a broken
      spirit;
   a broken and contrite heart, O God, you
      will not despise.

Second Reading   Hebrews 10:5-17

When Christ came into the world, he said,

"Sacrifices and offerings you have not
   desired,
but a body you have prepared for me;
in burnt offerings and sin offerings
you have taken no pleasure.
Then I said, 'Lo, I have come to do your
   will, O God,'
as it is written of me in the roll of the
   book."

When he said above, "You have neither desired nor taken pleasure in sacrifices and offerings and burnt offerings and sin offerings" (these are offered according to the law), then he added, "Lo, I have come to do your will." He abolishes the first in order to establish the second. And by that will we have been sanctified through the offering of the body of Jesus Christ once for all.

And every priest stands daily at his service, offering repeatedly the same sacrifices, which can never take away sins. But when Christ had offered for all time a single sacrifice for sins, he sat down at the right hand of God, then to wait until his enemies should be made a stool for his feet. For by a single offering he has perfected for all time those who are sanctified. And the Holy Spirit also bears witness to us; for after saying,

"This is the covenant that I will make
    with them
after those days, says the Lord:
I will put my laws on their hearts,
and write them on their minds,"
then he adds,
"I will remember their sins and their
    misdeeds no more."

Pause in silence. Try to experience within your heart this assurance of the Holy Spirit— and the deep peace and serene joy which come from knowing that he abides in us, that our sins are forgiven, that we have been made holy. With your heart lifted up to him, and your mind fixed on him, mentally repeat, in rhythm with your breathing, single words such as "holy," "you," "Lord," etc.

Responsorial

Alleluia. Alleluia.
Through the Spirit who has been given us,
alleluia,
our sins are forgiven
and we are made children of God,
alleluia.

We have received the Holy Spirit,
the Advocate,
alleluia,
whom the Father has sent in Jesus' name,
to abide with us,
alleluia,
and to teach us all truth.
Let us, therefore, love him,
and hold fast to him through that love
which is poured forth in our hearts,
alleluia,
through the Spirit who has been given us.
Alleluia. Alleluia. Alleluia.

Gospel Reading   John 14:15-17; 25-27

   If you love me, you will keep my
commandments. And I will pray the Father,
and he will give you another Counsellor, to
be with you for ever, even the Spirit of truth,
whom the world cannot receive, because it
neither sees him nor knows him; you know
him, for he dwells with you, and will be in
you.

   These things I have spoken to you, while
I am still with you. But the Counsellor, the
Holy Spirit, whom the Father will send in
my name, he will teach you all things, and
bring to your remembrance all that I have
said to you. Peace I leave with you; my

peace I give to you; not as the world gives do I give to you. Let not your hearts be troubled, neither let them be afraid.

Pause in silence. In spirit, join the band of Jesus' followers in the upper room. Look around at the people there, considering who they are and what they are destined to become. Listen to our Lord as he speaks, and experience for yourself the hope and strength and confidence to serve him which comes with his promise of the Spirit. Experience in yourself the peace which he imparts. Speak to our Lord as the thoughts and affections of your heart will direct.

General Intercessions

See pages 41-42.

Final Hymn

O breathe on me, Breath of God,
Fill me with life anew,
That I may love what thou dost love,
And do what thou wouldst do.

O breathe on me, Breath of God,
Until my heart is pure:
Until with thee I have one will
To do and to endure.

O breathe on me, Breath of God,
Till I am wholly thine,
Until this earthly part of me
Glows with thy fire divine.

O breathe on me, Breath of God,
So shall I never die,
But live with thee the perfect life,
Of thine eternity.

E. Hatch, from the Irish

A Month of Daily Readings

Before reading the Scriptures, pause for a few moments and direct your thoughts in love and obedience to the Holy Spirit who dwells within you and inspires your reading.

Opening Prayer

Open my heart, Holy Spirit, to receive your Word and enlighten my mind to understand it. Strengthen my will, Holy Spirit, to follow wherever you lead.

Read the day's passage—slowly, thoughtfully —in the company of the Holy Spirit who inspired it.

Concluding Prayer

I thank you, Holy Spirit, for your Word. Make it a living reality in my life—a constant guide at my side, a lamp for my feet and a light for my path. Let it mold my mind and shape my heart into the image of Christ my Lord, and in conformity to your holy will.

Date	Reading
1	Luke 1:26-38
2	Luke 1:39-56
3	Matthew 1:18-23

4	Luke 4:16-22
5	Luke 10:21-24
6	John 3:1-8
7	John 4:7-24
8	John 6:60-69
9	John 14:15-31
10	John 16:4-15
11	Matthew 28:16-20
12	Luke 24:36-49
13	Revelation 1:4-11
14	Revelation 4:1-11
15	1 Peter 1:1-12
16	2 Peter 1:16-21
17	1 John 2:20-27
18	1 John 3:22-24
19	1 John 4:1-6
20	1 John 4:7-16
21	1 John 5:6-12
22	James 4:1-10
23	Acts 8:26-40
24	Hebrews 10:19-31
25	Hebrews 12:1-13
26	Isaiah 11:1-9
27	Psalm 139
28	Wisdom 9:1-18
29	Daniel 2:20-23
30	Zephaniah 3:11-18
31	Judith 16:13-20

A Reading from St. Augustine

"Those who are begotten of God are led by the Spirit of God," says the Scripture. But do not think that you are drawn against your will—for the soul is drawn by love. You insist, "How do I believe voluntarily if I am drawn?" I tell you, they are the same thing—"to be willing," and, "to be drawn by delight." What is this "to be drawn by delight," you ask. It is as the Scriptures say: "Delight in the Lord, and he will give you your heart's desires." For the heart, too, has its delights. Shall the senses of the body have their pleasures, and the soul not? If the soul did not have its pleasures, it would not be written: "Humanity shall find hope in the shelter of your wings; they will be filled with the abundance of your house, and you will give them to drink of the torrent of your delight. For with you is the fountain of life; and in your light we shall see light."

Chaplet of the Holy Spirit

In the name of the Father and of the Son and of the Holy Spirit. Amen.

Recite an Act of Contrition.

The "Veni Creator" (page 37).

V. Send forth your Spirit, O Lord, and they shall be created.

R. And you will renew the face of the earth.

Let us pray:

O God, you instruct the hearts of the faithful by the light of the Holy Spirit: grant that through the same Holy Spirit we may have a right understanding in all things, and ever rejoice in his consolation. Through Christ our Lord. Amen.

The Mysteries

Say one Our Father, one Hail Mary, one Glory be..., seven times.

1. Jesus is conceived by the power of the Holy Spirit (Luke 1).
2. The Holy Spirit rests upon Jesus at his baptism by John (Matthew 3).
3. The Holy Spirit leads Jesus into the wilderness, to be tempted (Luke 4).

4. The Holy Spirit descends upon and abides in the Church (Acts 2).
5. The Holy Spirit lives in the souls of the just (Galatians 5; 1 Corinthians 6).

In the name of the Father and of the Son and of the Holy Spirit. Amen.

Traditional

Pauline
BOOKS & MEDIA

The Daughters of St. Paul operate book and media centers at the following addresses. Visit, call or write the one nearest you today, or find us on the World Wide Web, www.pauline.org

CALIFORNIA
3908 Sepulveda Blvd, Culver City, CA 90230   310-397-8676
5945 Balboa Avenue, San Diego, CA 92111   858-565-9181
46 Geary Street, San Francisco, CA 94108   415-781-5180

FLORIDA
145 S.W. 107th Avenue, Miami, FL 33174   305-559-6715

HAWAII
1143 Bishop Street, Honolulu, HI 96813   808-521-2731
Neighbor Islands call:
800-259-8463

ILLINOIS
172 North Michigan Avenue, Chicago, IL 60601   312-346-4228

LOUISIANA
4403 Veterans Memorial Blvd, Metairie, LA 70006   504-887-7631

MASSACHUSETTS
Rte. 1, 885 Providence Hwy, Dedham, MA 02026   781-326-5385

MISSOURI
9804 Watson Road, St. Louis, MO 63126   314-965-3512

NEW JERSEY
561 U.S. Route 1, Wick Plaza, Edison, NJ 08817   732-572-1200

NEW YORK
150 East 52nd Street, New York, NY 10022   212-754-1110
78 Fort Place, Staten Island, NY 10301   718-447-5071

OHIO
2105 Ontario Street, Cleveland, OH 44115   216-621-9427

PENNSYLVANIA
9171-A Roosevelt Blvd, Philadelphia, PA 19114   215-676-9494

SOUTH CAROLINA
243 King Street, Charleston, SC 29401   843-577-0175

TENNESSEE
4811 Poplar Avenue, Memphis, TN 38117   901-761-2987

TEXAS
114 Main Plaza, San Antonio, TX 78205   210-224-8101

VIRGINIA
1025 King Street, Alexandria, VA 22314   703-549-3806

CANADA
3022 Dufferin Street, Toronto, Ontario, Canada M6B 3T5
416-781-9131
1155 Yonge Street, Toronto, Ontario, Canada M4T 1W2
416-934-3440

¡También somos su fuente para libros, videos y música en español!